HISTORIC
COMMUNITIES

Life on a Plantation

Bobbie Kalman

 Crabtree Publishing Company

HISTORIC COMMUNITIES

Created by Bobbie Kalman

For Sybil Blyden with respect,
admiration, and fond memories

Editor-in-Chief
Bobbie Kalman

Research
April Fast

Writing team
Bobbie Kalman
Greg Nickles
Niki Walker

Managing editor
Lynda Hale

Editors
Niki Walker
Petrina Gentile
Greg Nickles

Photo research
Hannelore Sotzek

Computer design
Lynda Hale

Special thanks to
Cathy Grosfils; Maria DeOliveira; Dr. Marvin Dulaney;
Holly Watters, Kim Tuck, and Robert M. Hicklin Jr., Inc.;
The University of North Carolina at Chapel Hill; Penn Center, Inc.;
Professor Fred Drake; Loyd Hall Plantation; Houmas House
Plantation and Gardens; Nottoway Plantation; Oak Alley
Plantation; San Francisco Plantation; Kent House; Belle Air
Plantation; Destrehan Plantation; Gunston Hall Plantation;
Boone Hall Plantation; and Evelynton Plantation

Consultant
Julie Richter, Historian,
Colonial Williamsburg Foundation

Illustrations
Barbara Bedell: pages 6-7, 25
Antoinette "Cookie" DeBiasi: pages 14, 23

Separations and film
Dot 'n Line Image Inc.

Printer
Worzalla Publishing Company

Crabtree Publishing Company

350 Fifth Avenue
Suite 3308
New York
N.Y. 10118

360 York Road, RR 4
Niagara-on-the-Lake
Ontario, Canada
L0S 1J0

73 Lime Walk
Headington
Oxford OX3 7AD
United Kingdom

Cataloging in Publication Data
Kalman, Bobbie
  Life on a plantation
(Historic communities series)
Includes index.
ISBN 0-86505-435-5 (library bound) ISBN 0-86505-465-7 (pbk.)

This book examines what life was like on the plantations that
existed in the southern United States into the nineteenth century.

1. Plantation life - Southern States - Juvenile literature. 2. Southern
States - Social life and customs - 1775-1865 - Juvenile literature.
I. Title. II. Series: Kalman, Bobbie. Historic Communities.

F213.K35 1996   j975'.03   96-44507
                                                CIP

Contents

What is a plantation?

The beautiful home above was once part of a large farm in the southern United States. Many such farms, or **plantations**, existed 150 years ago. They specialized in growing one valuable crop, such as tobacco, cotton, or rice. Plantations were also places where many people lived, worked, and struggled to survive.

Early plantations

The first plantations were built in the 1600s by British settlers. The owners of plantations were called **planters**. A planter, his family, and a few workers ran an early farm, growing crops to sell in Britain, North America, and other places around the world. Over time, some planter families grew rich from their harvests. They added more land to their farms and built large, fancy homes.

U.S.A., 1854
☐ slavery not allowed
■ slavery allowed
☐ undecided about slavery

Until the Civil War in the 1860s, each state had its own laws about slavery. At that time, slavery was legal in many southern states, including Texas, Louisiana, Georgia, and Mississippi. States that did not allow slavery included New York, Michigan, Pennsylvania, and California. Some areas, called **territories,** *were not yet states. In 1854 they were given the choice of whether or not to allow slavery.*

Slavery

Today, plantations are remembered for their rich crops, wealthy owners, and fancy homes, but they are also remembered for **slavery**. Slavery is the practice of owning human beings and forcing them to work without pay. Many planters grew rich because of slavery, but countless people suffered and died as a result of it.

The practice of slavery is wrong, not just because of the violence with which slaves were treated, but because it is wrong to think of people as property. Today, slavery is illegal in the United States, but between the 1600s and 1865, planters forced millions of people to live and work as slaves on the plantations.

Around a plantation

Each plantation was a little different from the others. Some were very small with only a few workers, and some were enormous with hundreds of slaves. Most plantations, such as the one pictured here, supported the planter's family and between 20 and 40 slaves. Many different buildings, animals, and pieces of equipment were needed to keep a plantation running.

1. The planter and his family lived in the largest home, called the **Big House**.
2. Meals for the planter's family were prepared in a kitchen separate from the Big House.
3. In the spinning house, slaves carded wool and spun it into yarn.
4. Cloth was woven at the weaving house.
5. Clothes were made in the sewing house.
6. The slave **quarters**, or homes, were built at the back of the property so the slaves were close to the fields in which they worked.
7. A house was used for candle and soap-making.
8. **Tallow**, or fat, was melted in the soap kettle.
9. Clothing was colored in the dye house.
10. Iron tools and horseshoes were made in the blacksmith shop.
11. In the carpentry shop, items such as beams, planks, furniture, and coffins were made.
12. The barn and stables sheltered the horses, cows, sheep, turkeys, and chickens.
13. Laundry from the Big House was done in the wash house.
14. The ice house preserved milk and fresh meat.
15. A well or spring house provided water.
16. A smoke house was used to preserve meats.
17. The carriage house stored the planter's coaches and carriages.
18. Boots and shoes were made in the shoemaker's shop.

Plantation jobs

To keep a plantation running smoothly, each person had a set of jobs to do. The slaves did the hardest, most unpleasant work, whereas the planter family supervised and enjoyed the rewards of the slaves' labor.

The planter family

The planter, or **master**, was the head of the plantation. He managed the money and farm work and told family members and slaves what they could and could not do. On smaller plantations, he often worked with his slaves in the fields.

The planter's wife managed the Big House. She gave directions to the slaves on meal preparation, cleaning, and watching the children. Some wives also supervised the women's workshops. If the planter's children were old enough, they also helped manage the workers.

House slaves

Cooks, maids, nurses, and butlers were house slaves. Some did general chores such as cooking and cleaning, and others waited on the planter's family. There were many jobs to do in the Big House.

Skilled jobs

Large plantations often had workshops in which skilled slaves made clothes, shoes, and farm tools. Skilled slaves included tradespeople such as blacksmiths, millers, weavers, tailors, and shoemakers. In many cases, these slaves knew two or three trades.

Field work

More slaves worked in the fields than at any other place on the farm. These slaves were men, women, and older children who spent long hours in the hot fields plowing, sowing seeds, pulling weeds, and harvesting crops. Field workers also tended crops such as corn, potatoes, and wheat, which were eaten by people at the plantation.

Overseers and slave drivers

Overseers were white men hired to supervise the field workers and, sometimes, the skilled slaves. They watched for mistakes, punished the slaves, and made sure they worked quickly. An overseer also inspected the tools, livestock, and buildings. Sometimes a planter made one of his trusted field slaves a **slave driver**. The driver was expected to watch over other slaves and punish them while he worked alongside them in the fields.

(opposite page) Most planters were men with families, but some plantations were owned and run by widows or single men or women. (below) Each day, slaves had to feed and give water to the planter's livestock. Sometimes slaves raised livestock of their own.

Plantation workers

In the 1600s, most of the workers on the plantations were **indentured servants**. Indentured servants were people who wanted to come to North America to build a new life for themselves and their families, but they could not afford the voyage. Many came from Britain, and a few came from Europe and Africa. These people offered to work on plantations in exchange for their trip across the Atlantic Ocean. They worked several years before their **indenture**, or debt, to the planter was considered paid. Once their indenture was paid, they were free to work wherever they chose.

Fewer willing workers

By the 1700s, very few people chose to live the harsh life of an indentured servant. To replace indentured workers, plantation owners began bringing slaves from Africa. By the late 1700s, slaves were doing most of the work on plantations. Unlike indentured servants, few slaves had a chance to gain freedom. Most spent their entire life working in brutal conditions with very few rights or rewards.

Unfair treatment of slaves

Some slave owners treated their workers very cruelly. At that time, the laws did little to improve the treatment of slaves. Although some areas had laws against mistreating and injuring slaves, these crimes still happened and often went unpunished. A law passed in 1808 made it illegal to bring slaves to America, but people continued to do so. Slaves worked on plantations until 1865, when slavery finally became illegal.

The slave trade

During the years plantations existed, millions of people became slave workers. Some slaves were Africans who were captured and brought to North America. Others were the children of these Africans. Slaves were purchased and forced to work on plantations, in factories, and at family homes. The buying and selling of slaves is called the **slave trade**.

A terrible journey

Slave hunters made money by kidnapping Africans and selling them as slaves. Armed with whips and guns, they forced their prisoners onto crowded ships that sailed across the Atlantic Ocean. For most of the two-month trip, the captives were chained up in the dark, filthy cargo space below the ship's deck. Some slave hunters beat their prisoners and burned marks into their skin to identify them. Many prisoners died of illness, abuse, and depression.

When the ships arrived in North America, the new slaves were terrified. After being kidnapped and tortured, the Africans found themselves in a strange new land where they knew no one. They could not understand the language of their captors, so they did not know where they would be taken or what was going to happen to them.

Slave auctions

The captives were put up for sale at a **slave auction**. The buyers and sellers of slaves had little concern for their feelings or happiness. Parents and children were split apart and sold to different owners. Most never saw one another again.

These people are preparing for a slave auction. The slaves cling to their loved ones while the white traders casually discuss prices. Young, healthy men were sold first, women of child-bearing age second, and all others, including children, were auctioned off last.

Planters and their wives were expected to act like perfect gentlemen and ladies. Many dressed in fine fashions and practiced strict manners.

The planters

Many planter families pictured themselves as graceful lords and ladies, such as those living in the castles of Europe. They believed that men should be strong, educated leaders and that women should know how to run the family home and entertain guests. To show off their wealth and good manners, planter families held and attended fancy dinners, dances, and other expensive events. Many families competed to see who could hold the most lavish dinners and parties.

Daily life

In day-to-day life, however, most planter families were not like European nobility. Owners of small plantations could not afford to keep many slaves. These planters worked hard in the fields and had little time or money to live like lords or ladies.

Racial prejudice

Few planters felt it was wrong to keep black people as slaves because they were **prejudiced** against them. Prejudice is a negative opinion about people of a different race, religion, or background. People often fear others who are different because they do not understand them. This fear can lead to prejudice. Most planters thought that, because they were white, they were better than the slaves, who were black. They did not feel it was wrong to take away the freedom of the slaves, deny them an education, separate their family members, and even torture them.

Keeping control

On large plantations, there were far more slaves than whites. Some planters feared that their slaves would rebel against them with violence. Different planters had different ways of avoiding rebellions.

Some planters felt that severe punishment and shows of power were the best ways to keep slaves from becoming disobedient. They gave their slaves brutal beatings and chained, burned, and maimed them. Other owners threatened to split apart slave families and sell members to different plantations if someone misbehaved. A few planters used violence and threats only as a last resort. They believed that if slaves were happy, they would work hard and not rebel.

Many slaves learned to live in fear of their masters. They hated the way they were treated, but without weapons, they had little power to stop the abuse they received.

The slave community

Slaves needed their owners' permission to marry. Most masters encouraged marriage because they believed that married slaves were not likely to run away.

Having a family brought happiness, but it also brought fear. At any time, a family member could be sold. Some masters sold family members as a punishment.

Slaves on a plantation formed a community apart from that of the planter family. Slaves relied on one another for emotional support, entertainment, and extra food and supplies. They also worked together to preserve their customs and protect one another from their master.

Not all slaves cooperated with one another, however. For a reward, some slaves spied for the master and betrayed runaways or those who were planning to rebel. In the 1700s especially, many American-born Christian slaves would not associate with those who had recently arrived from Africa because they found their customs strange.

Keeping their culture

Planters made African-born slaves learn English and practice Christianity. The slaves learned European ways, but in the quarters, many still celebrated African customs. They were not encouraged to read or write, so knowledge was passed on to others through stories and songs.

Secret resistance

Most masters did not want their slaves to have an education because they feared the slaves would use knowledge against them. Many slaves learned in secret, however. At night, some learned to read in hidden places called **pit schools**. Slaves who believed in Christianity sometimes ran **invisible churches**. Only slaves knew about these churches, whose members held secret meetings in the forest. White church services stressed obedience, but invisible churches taught slaves about the happiness and equality they would find in heaven.

Escaping to freedom

Many slaves helped one another plan an escape to freedom. Some belonged to the **Underground Railroad**, a secret organization that gave runaway slaves food, transportation, and places to hide. Members passed coded messages to runaways through songs, stories, and signs such as notches in trees.

Many planters allowed their slaves to sing, dance, visit, or play music on Sundays and holidays. Some slaves did extra work on these days in order to earn a little money.

Slaves were watched closely while they worked, but they found a little peace and privacy in their quarters.

Children at the plantation

Wealthier planters wanted their daughters to learn to sing or play a musical instrument. These "ladylike" skills entertained guests and impressed potential husbands.

(opposite page, top) Many slave children worked in the fields.

(opposite page, bottom) These girls are grinding corn. Coarse ground corn, or cornmeal, was a staple of slave diets.

Many children were born and raised on plantations. Sometimes young white and black children played together. The children of planters, however, led very different lives than those of slave children. Plantation owners raised their children to take over the family business. A child born to a slave was the property of the planter. Older slave children were either put to work on the plantation or sold to another farm.

The planter's children

Younger children had few responsibilities. They spent much of their time at play, either in the Big House or romping around the plantation. The planters, however, wanted their children to learn to act like young ladies and gentlemen. As they grew older, children took part in more of the adult events such as dances and dinner parties. They were also taught how to run the plantation.

The children of slaves

Many babies died before being born because their mothers were weak and tired. Some babies died later as a result of illnesses or because they did not get enough healthy food.

Young slave children were often free to run and play around the plantation, but their life of "freedom" did not last long. They saw their parents being yelled at and beaten. Sometimes they watched as a parent was dragged away in chains to be sold. As the children grew older, the planter gave them more duties and chores. Children between the ages of eight and twelve were ordered to do the work of adults in the fields or the Big House. Some were sold to other plantations.

Education for some—not for others

Planters wanted their children to be educated, but they had different expectations for boys and girls. Both were taught reading, writing, and arithmetic. Boys, however, were expected to learn other subjects such as geography and history. Many boys studied only until they were teenagers, but some went on to attend a college or **military academy**. To prepare them for marriage, girls were taught homemaking skills and proper manners.

Most slave children were not allowed to attend school, although a few slaves were taught to read and write by a kind master, his wife or children, or another slave. Slave parents taught their children another type of lesson—how to behave around whites in order to avoid punishment.

As it was then

The photographs on these pages were taken in the nineteenth century. They are actual pictures of slaves who lived on plantations.

These workers are finally returning to their quarters after a long day in the cotton fields. Their work day ended at sundown, but the slaves worked late into the night doing their own chores in the quarters.

Slaves were given only one set of clothing and one pair of shoes each year. Clothing was loose-fitting so that a slave could move easily while working. The clothes were made from a coarser cloth than that used for the planter family's clothing. If their shoes or clothing wore out, slaves had to do without new ones until the following year. Most went barefoot during the summer and saved their shoes for cooler weather.

Most slave homes were crowded. Sometimes ten or more people shared a tiny one-room cabin. Many planters gave slaves cooking tools and a mattress for sleeping. Slaves did extra work to get furniture or they made it themselves.

The plantation owner often insisted on naming the children of his slaves. The name he chose was usually used only at work. In the quarters, the child had another name, which was given by his or her parents. This name was kept secret. Since many families were split apart, the name was often a child's only tie to the family.

There were no nurseries for the children of slaves. Often, they were cared for by an older child or an elderly woman while their parents worked.

Planters did not want young children in the fields because they distracted their parents from their work. This picture shows a baby in the fields while her mother is working, but it must have been a rare situation.

The Big House

The Big House was the center of life and activity for the planter and his family. They ate, slept, played games, hosted parties, and relaxed in the home's fancy rooms.

Working in the house

House slaves rose before sunrise to lay out the family's clothing and prepare the morning meals. Nurses watched the children, and maids and cooks spent the day cooking, cleaning, and attending to guests. Some maids served a member of the planter's family throughout the day.

The living conditions of house slaves were better than those of other workers. House slaves wore the family's old clothes and ate their leftover food. Many house slaves were lonely, however, because they always worked alone or silently by their master's side, away from the other slaves.

The planter's wife, known as the **mistress**, *instructs a slave on setting the table for guests. (below) A house slave prepares the parlor for the planter family's evening of entertainment.*

Entertaining guests

Most planters liked to entertain guests, especially in the evenings after supper. People read stories and poems aloud or listened to music played by the planter's daughters. Sometimes the men went into another room to smoke, drink, and discuss politics. These activities were considered inappropriate for the women, who were left to chat and drink tea.

Christmas celebrations

In December the slaves helped decorate the Big House for Christmas. No expense was spared in decking the home with wreaths, ribbons, and green boughs. Some planters welcomed their slaves into the Big House on Christmas Day and gave them small gifts. Some also allowed their slaves to visit neighboring plantations. In the evening, masters and slaves held separate Christmas dinners.

Guests from a neighboring plantation arrive at the Big House in carriages. Many planter families also traveled by boat.

The field workers

Work in the fields was hot, dirty, and tiring, as slaves spent hours hunched over in the hot sun. The field workers tended the cotton, tobacco, or rice crops in addition to growing food crops and caring for livestock.

A long working day

Field slaves were awakened before sunrise by a **caller**. The caller walked through the quarters blowing a cow horn. By the time the sunrise horn was blown, the workers were already in the fields. They worked as long as there was daylight. In the summer, they often began working before five in the morning and did not return home until past eight o'clock in the evening!

Little chance to rest

Slaves were allowed a short lunch break during the day, but many went all day with little food or rest. On some plantations, even a quick stretch to ease a sore back was forbidden and brought the crack of the overseer's whip.

A wealthy planter stopped by the fields once a day to watch the workers and give orders to his overseer. He then returned to the Big House.

Plantation crops

Workers spent most of their time caring for **cash crops**, which were grown and sold for profit. Most plantations specialized in growing one of the following crops:

Tobacco was grown in Virginia and North Carolina. It was the most common, profitable plantation crop until the late 1700s, when cotton became more popular. Tobacco plants required a lot of care. Each morning, the slaves removed the grubs that ate the tobacco leaves. When the plants were ready for harvesting, the leaves were picked, dried, and packed into barrels for shipping.

Cotton was grown in the Deep South, in states such as Alabama, Georgia, and Louisiana. Cotton grows on bushes, in clusters called **bolls**. When the bolls ripened, they were plucked out of their prickly pods. Picking cotton was hard work that made the slaves' fingers bleed. A **cotton gin** was a machine used to remove the seeds from the cotton fibers before the cotton was pressed into bales for shipping.

Rice was grown in South Carolina. Slaves dreaded being sold to a rice plantation. Working in flooded fields, or **paddies**, all day caused skin problems and infections. Small water bugs bit at the slaves' legs, sometimes causing illness.

Busy harvests

Crops were usually harvested between mid-August and Christmas. The vast fields of ripe plants had to be harvested quickly. Planters ordered all available workers into the fields to pick, gather, and transport the crops to the barns and workshops. Many slaves worked days without sleep or free time.

After a crop was harvested, it had to be prepared quickly for use or storage. Corn was husked, or **shucked**. Wheat was stored in the barn and **threshed** to separate the grains and chaff. Cotton was run through the cotton gin to remove seeds from the useful fibers. Tobacco plants were dried and their leaves removed for storage through the winter.

Slaughtering

In the late fall, usually after the first frost, field slaves helped slaughter the livestock and prepare meat for the winter. Men did the butchering, and women used the animal fat for cooking and making candles and soap.

The meat was preserved by smoking it in the smoke house or storing it in barrels of salt water, called **brine**. The smoke house was also used to store the preserved meats. By the end of slaughtering time, the building was packed with hams, turkeys, sausages, and bacon for the planter's family. The planter locked the smoke-house door to keep his workers from stealing the valuable meat.

Winter work

Although the weather cooled in winter, it was not too cold for working outdoors. Planters ordered their field workers to clean up the fields and yard. Tools and equipment were fixed and stored, barns were cleaned, fences were mended, and horses were shod. Necessary repairs were made to the Big House.

Slaves pluck a chicken they raised for themselves. Its meat will give the family a good meal, and the feathers will be stuffed into a mattress.

These young women are husking corn to be dried and stored for winter.

Skilled labor

Coachmen *drove the planter's carriage. When they went to other plantations, they had a chance to talk to the slaves who lived there. They shared the news they heard with slaves at their own plantation. (below) This woman is carding wool in the spinning house.*

Most planters provided their slaves with bare necessities such as clothing, shoes, and tools. Plantations with lots of slaves often had workshops and skilled laborers to make these items. Making goods on the plantation was cheaper then buying them elsewhere. Skilled workers also made cloth, soap, and some tools, which saved the planter money.

Spinning, weaving, and sewing

Skilled women made cloth, clothing, and sacks. In the spinning house, wool and flax were carded and then spun into thread or yarn with a spinning wheel. A loom in the weaving house was used to weave threads into sheets of cloth. Women in the sewing house stitched clothes by hand for the other slaves. All this work made the women's hands painfully sore.

Horses and coaches

Horses and coaches were symbols of a planter's wealth. Several men cared for these prized possessions. A **coachman** was a driver who also looked after the carriage house, where coaches and carriages were kept. The blacksmith forged horseshoes, parts for the coaches, and iron tools for the rest of the plantation.

Other shops and houses

Carpentry and shoemaker's shops were found on many plantations. The carpenter crafted wooden tools, furniture, and parts for tools and farm machines. The shoemaker made footwear for everyone on the farm.

Women washed the planter family's clothing at the laundry house. They shook out the clean laundry and hung it outside to dry.

At the carpentry workshop, this log will be cut into a square beam. The beam, along with many more, will be used to build the planter's new barn.

The fight for freedom

Slaves did not have the power to end slavery, but many showed their anger by disobeying their owners, working slowly, and secretly breaking equipment to stop farm work. While slaves protested against slavery, many free blacks and whites worked to make slavery illegal.

Escaping slavery

Every year, a few slaves escaped and fled north. Attempting an escape was very dangerous. An owner whose slave was missing gathered a band of helpers and chased the fleeing slave on horseback. Vicious hounds were set loose to track and attack the runaway. Slaves were punished severely or even killed if they were caught.

The Civil War begins

In 1860, President Abraham Lincoln was elected. He wanted to limit slavery to the southern states, but planters wanted slavery to be legal throughout the country. The states in the South decided to separate from the United States, but the North did not want to let them go. In 1861, the Civil War broke out between the North and South. People who sided with the South were known as **Confederates**; those who fought for the North in the **Union Army** were called **Yankees**.

The Emancipation Proclamation

By 1862, the North appeared to be losing the war. To create problems for the Confederate states and help the North win, Lincoln issued the **Emancipation Proclamation**. On January 1, 1863, the Proclamation freed all slaves living in the states that were at war with the No

Although the slaves were set free, they still faced prejudice and unfair treatment throughout the United States and Canada. Today, many people still struggle for equality and human rights.

War on the plantations

Much of the war was fought in the South, in plantation fields and nearby woods. Some Big Houses were used as army headquarters or hospitals. Thousands of people were killed and many plantations ruined. After the Emancipation Proclamation, some slaves chose to stay on the farms. Others joined the Yankees and helped them grow food, make supplies, and fight the Confederates.

The end of the war and slavery

In 1865, the Union Army won the Civil War. The United States Constitution was altered to include the **Thirteenth Amendment**, making slavery illegal. Not many plantations were rebuilt because planters could not find people to perform the tiring jobs formerly done by slaves. In recent years, a few Big Houses have been restored as museums, reminding people of the wealth once enjoyed by the planters.

Glossary

cash crop A plant grown to be sold for profit rather than for the farmer's use

culture The customs, beliefs, and arts of a group of people

Emancipation Proclamation An announcement that declared freedom for all slaves living in states that were at war with the Union. Made by President Abraham Lincoln, it was put into effect January 1, 1863.

free blacks Describing African Americans who, at the time of slavery, were not slaves

nobility A group of people who have high social ranking or titles, such as dukes, dutchesses, barons, and baronesses

overseer A person hired to supervise and punish slaves in the place of the planter; often found on large plantations

prejudice A negative judgement made about a group of people based on their race, religion, or background

resistance The act of opposing something or someone

Thirteenth Amendment A change, made in 1865, to the United States Constitution. The Thirteenth Amendment made slavery illegal throughout the United States.

tradespeople People skilled in a particular craft or trade, such as carpentry or blacksmithing

Index

Acknowledgments

Photographs and reproductions

Carmack Papers, #PA-1414, Vol. 1/Southern Historical Collection, Library of the University of North Carolina at Chapel Hill: pages 20 (top, bottom), 21 (all)

Chicago Historical Society (1957.0027): pages 12-13

Colonial Williamsburg Foundation: pages 8, 9, 15, 16 (both), 17 (both), 18, 19, 22 (both), 25, 27 (both), 28 (both), 29 (both)

Evelynton Plantation: page 23

Houmas House Plantation and Gardens: page 4

Robert M. Hicklin Jr., Inc., Spartanburg, SC/various Private Collections: Detail from *Plantation Economy in the Old South*: cover, page 5; *The Sunny South*: pages 10-11; Detail from *In the Cottonfields*: page 19; *The Cotton Pickers*: page 24; *Taking Cotton to Market*: page 26

The Metropolitan Museum of Art, Gift of Erving and Joyce Wolf, (1982.443.3) Detail: pages 30-31

Oak Alley Plantation, Vacherie, LA: title page

Penn School Collection/Penn Center, Inc., St. Helena Island, SC: page 20 (middle)

1 2 3 4 5 6 7 8 9 0   Printed in the U.S.A.   6 5 4 3 2 1 0 9 8 7